In his invaluable book, Christian Buckholz, one of the great drummers in the Lennie Tristano scene, lays out for us some of the concepts that Lennie used in his teaching of rhythm.

Thanks to Christian for making these teachings available for the first time!

Dave Frank

Associate Professor of Piano

Berklee College of Music

Director, Dave Frank School of Jazz, NYC

DRUMS

My Studies with Lennie Tristano
&
A Drummer's Escapades

By

Christian Buckholz

ALSO AVAILABLE:

<u>The Ultimate Study in Independence</u> – An organized plan to develop your independence. Every exercise grooves. Applications in Funk, Fusion, Jazz and Latin.

By Christian Buchkholz and Ronnie Ciago

<u>Connections</u> – Beginning to advanced drum studies in Rock, Latin, and Jazz. Students can begin and go beyond with the material

By Christian Buckholz and Rod Thomas

<u>Rhythm Sketches</u> – Jazz excerpts, including intros, outros, fill and short solos for complete drum set.

By Christian Buckholz

<u>Drum Rhythm Series</u> – Available as separate volumes and complete in 1 Volume:

<u>Book 1: Rhythms for Every Instrument</u>

<u>Book 2: Main Rudiments of Drumming</u>

<u>Book 3: Rock, Jazz and Punk for Drumset</u>

By Christian Buckholz and Rod Thomas

SOLD BY:

P.C. Music

8196 Ambach Way

Hypoluxo, FL 33462

<u>www.drumthis.com</u>

DRUMS – My Studies with Lennie Tristano & A Drummer's Escapades

By Christian Buckholz

Copyright 2019

All Rights Reserved

Printed in the United States of America

Acknowledgements

I would like to thank my wife, Susan, for her love, help, kindness and support, all of these 41 years of marriage.

Next, my associate, friend, drummer and computer expert, Rod Thomas, who has contributed to so many of our books over the years. A special thanks also to his wife, Kelly, for this and previous thoughtful, artful and terrific covers. Thanks too for their kind remarks about my Sunday dinners—all two that I know how to make.

Kudos to Lennie Tristano! He made me a better person and a better musician.

I thank God for my three daughters, Dawn, Erika and Colette, and for my ex-wife, Jeck.

Lennie Tristano taught drummers to play the way he felt they should play. I agreed with him, but I noticed that when I played out with Sonny Dallas, he wanted me to play with a triplet feel, but with Lennie, the feel was with the "let" count all the way over to the right. Thus:

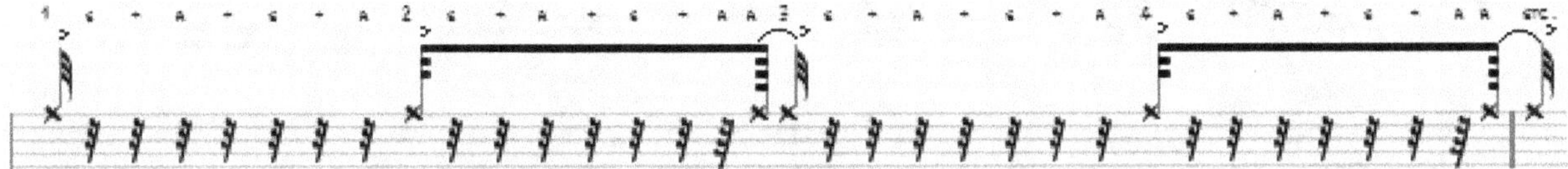

Figure 1

Lennie's reasoning for this was to leave an open space for the soloist between each quarter pulse. I loved the feel with or without a soloist. At any rate, try it, you may like it. It may take a few months or so, but stick with it. Remember, the left hand is LIGHTER than the right—it just provokes the soloist, and is, along with your right foot, your improvised line, but first, just use your left and right hands.

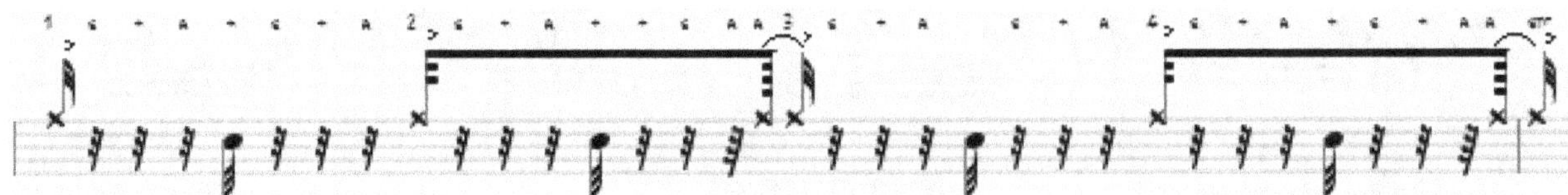

Figure 2.

Notice how close the so called "let" count is—a 64th note at the end of counts 2 and 4. That's why I put the mark ⌒ on top of those two notes. It's not a verifiable musical notation. I am showing, with this sign ⌒, that these two notes are very closely spaced— a 64th note apart.

Now try this:

Figure 3.

Again, the sign ⌢ on top of the last of 2 and 4 is just to indicate that the last two counts are 64th counts. I just thought it would be more understandable and easier to locate the 64th note—commonly called the "skip" note (if it were part of a triplet).

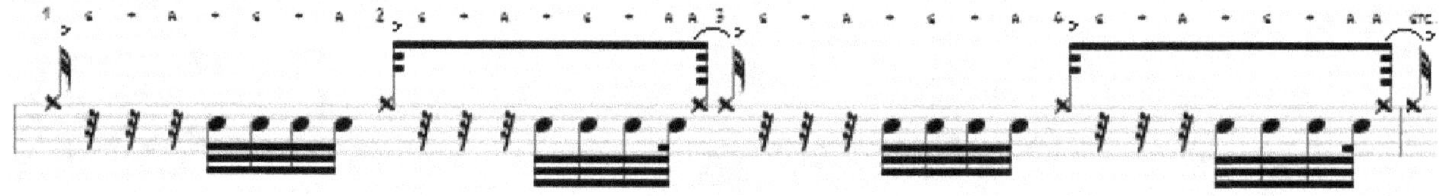

Figure 4.

Take your time mastering these exercises, perhaps a month or so. If you are uncertain about your "Let" stroke (the 64th leading to counts 3, and also 1 of the next measure), practice it before moving forward.

These exercises are intended to help you acquire the feel of the "Let" count, the 64th note (in our case), all the way to the right-- a totally different feel! I agree with Lennie on this. As you can see, this was important, but I must admit, rare.

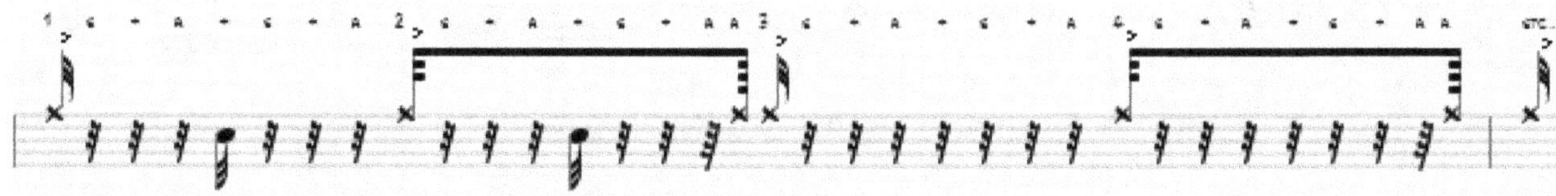

Figure 5: figure 2 with figure 1.

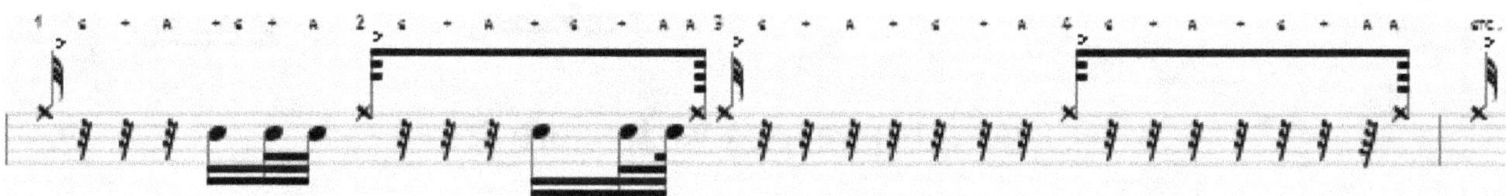

Figure 6: figure 3 with figure 1.

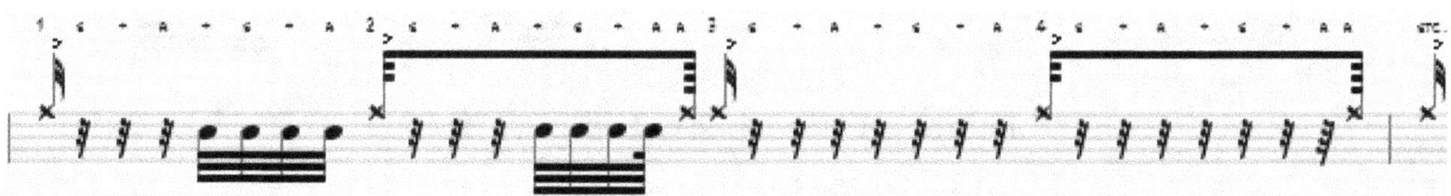

Figure 7: figure 4 with figure 1.

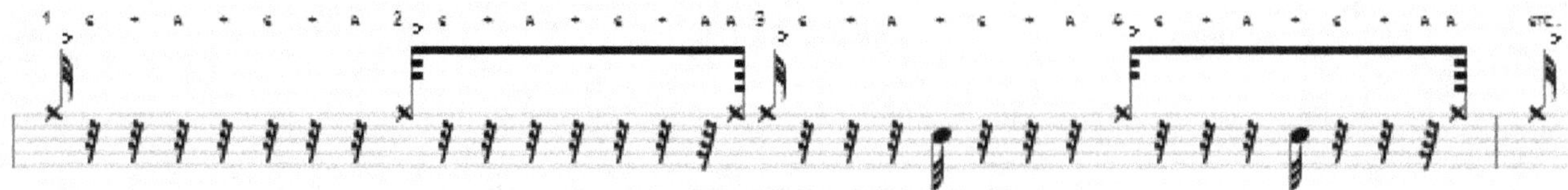

Figure 8: figure 1 with figure 2.

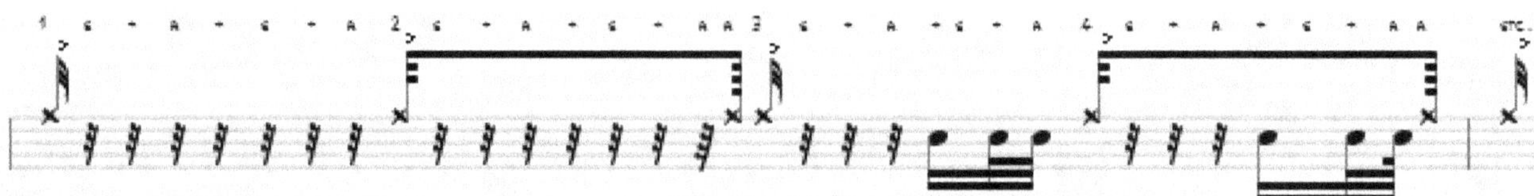

Figure 9: figure 1 with figure 3.

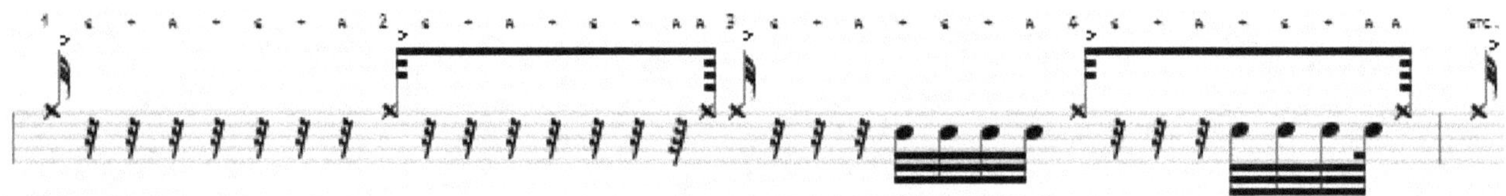

Figure 10: figure 1 with figure 4.

Figure 11: figure 2 with figure 3.

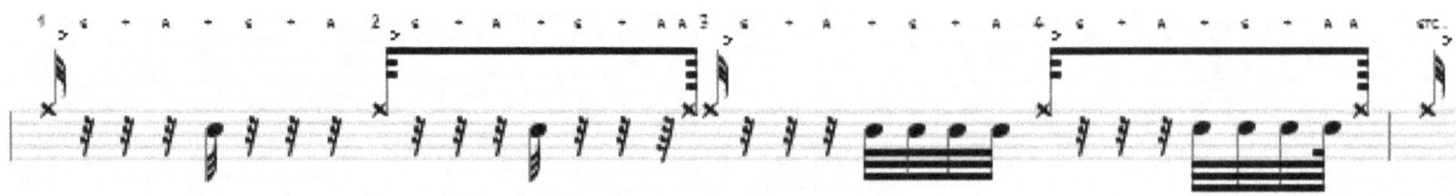

Figure 12: figure 2 with figure 4.

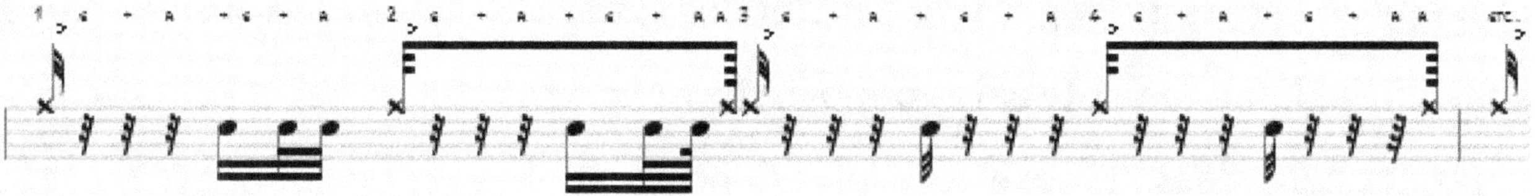

Figure 13: figure 3 with figure 2.

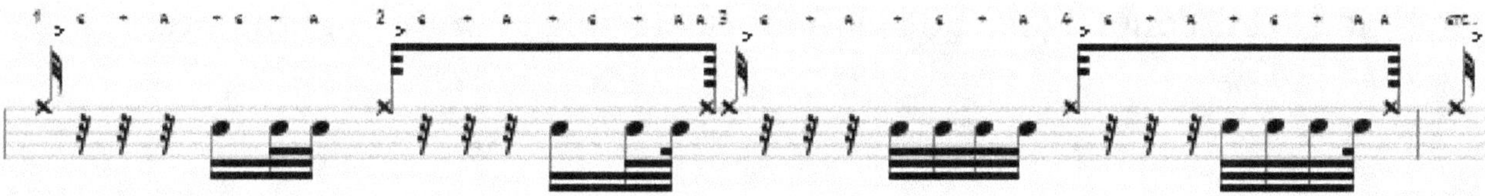

Figure 14: figure 3 with figure 4.

Figure 15: figure 4 with figure 2.

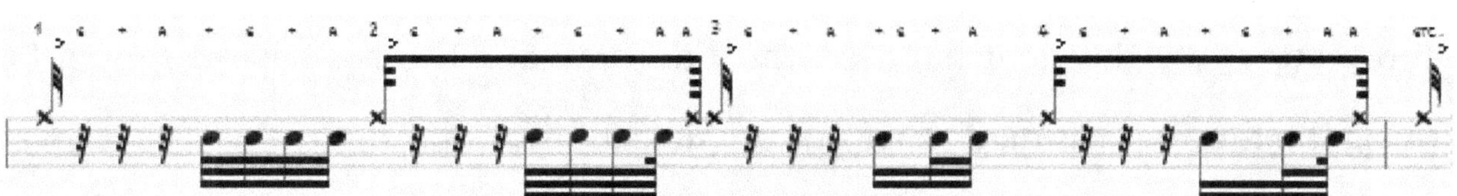

Figure 16: figure 4 with figure 3.

Again, the purpose of these exercises is to play the "let" counts of the ride cymbal all the way over to the right while maintaining the left hand in its proper place. None of the left hand notes are to move from their rightful place. Be careful that your right hand doesn't move your left. Concentrate heavily on counts 1, 2, 3, 4.

These exercises, for all advanced players, are mainly to prepare you to play your right hand "Let" count against other figures, starting with the eighth note.

Back to the "man." There were areas of Jazz drumming that Lennie Tristano expected you to perfect as a drummer. They were, of course, "Time" (playing with a metronome); "Music" (listening to and singing with records, first Frank Sinatra, then Lester Young, then Charlie Parker—Byrd, to us); putting the notes in the right place with the hands and feet, and moving the last note on the ride cymbal after 2 & 4 as far to the right as possible—a 64th note.

Now, on to the feet! The left foot plays the Hi-Hat on beats 2 and 4. It should be almost buried by the right hand on the ride cymbal. The right hand should be driving the time with as much space as possible in the "Let" count, a 64th note away or as far away as you possibly can, depending on the tempo and your facility. The four pulses should be equally loud. Simply put, the counts 1, 2, 3, 4, should be played evenly and hard. The right foot and the left hand do almost all the improvising (under the sound of the right hand) while the right hand varies occasionally, still with a strong feeling of four.

The previous exercises were to aid you in placing the 64th "Let" count on your ride cymbal. Now let's study the works. Remember, these are exercises only. Your improvising comes from your knowledge and personal feel of the tune. Constantly learn tunes, especially those of your bag. At least learn forms, "A A B A"— 8 measures, 8 measures repeated, leading to the bridge which is 8 measures, then 8 of the original 8 measures with a lead-in to the improvisation, usually part of the last 8. Of course there are other forms—"A A B A C," "A B A B C," and so on. Check them out while you learn the form of the tunes you play.

Now begin, without bass drum.

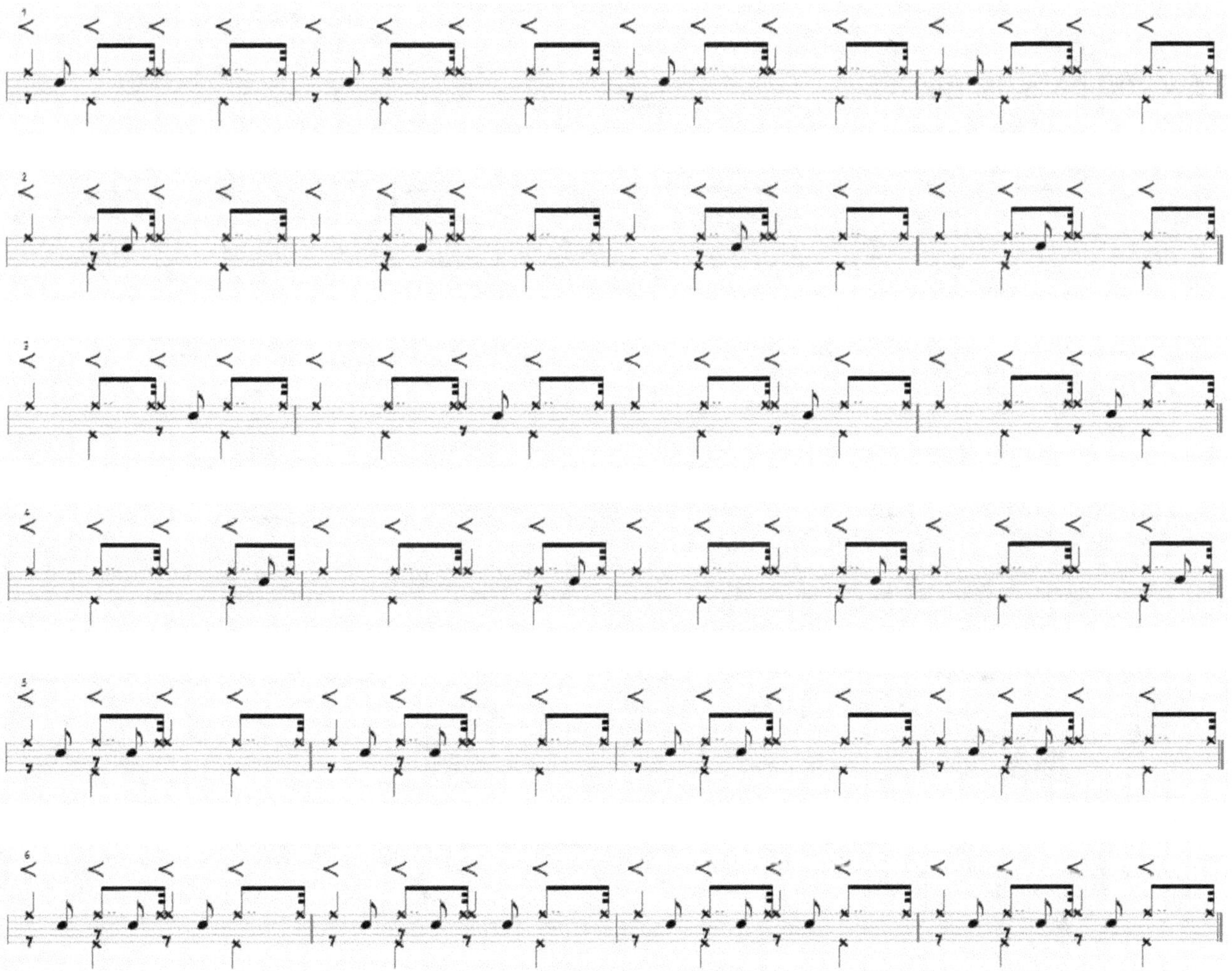

Maintain accents throughout on 1, 2, 3, 4. After you spend a good amount of time (about a month or so), try the following ride cymbal, snare and bass patterns. Notice the counts are different here, and as a result, you can play at least twice as fast. Repeat each 4 measures preceded by 4 measures of time, i.e.:

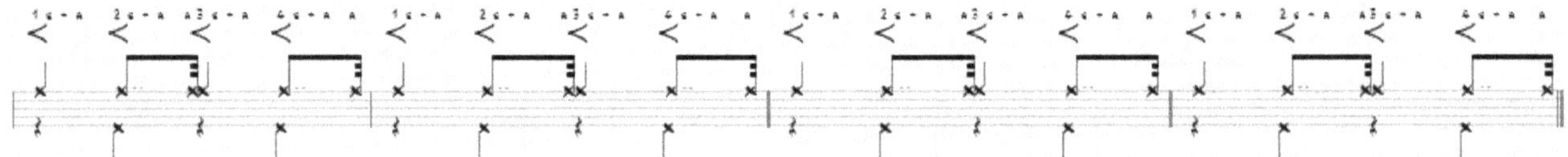

Now add bass drum.

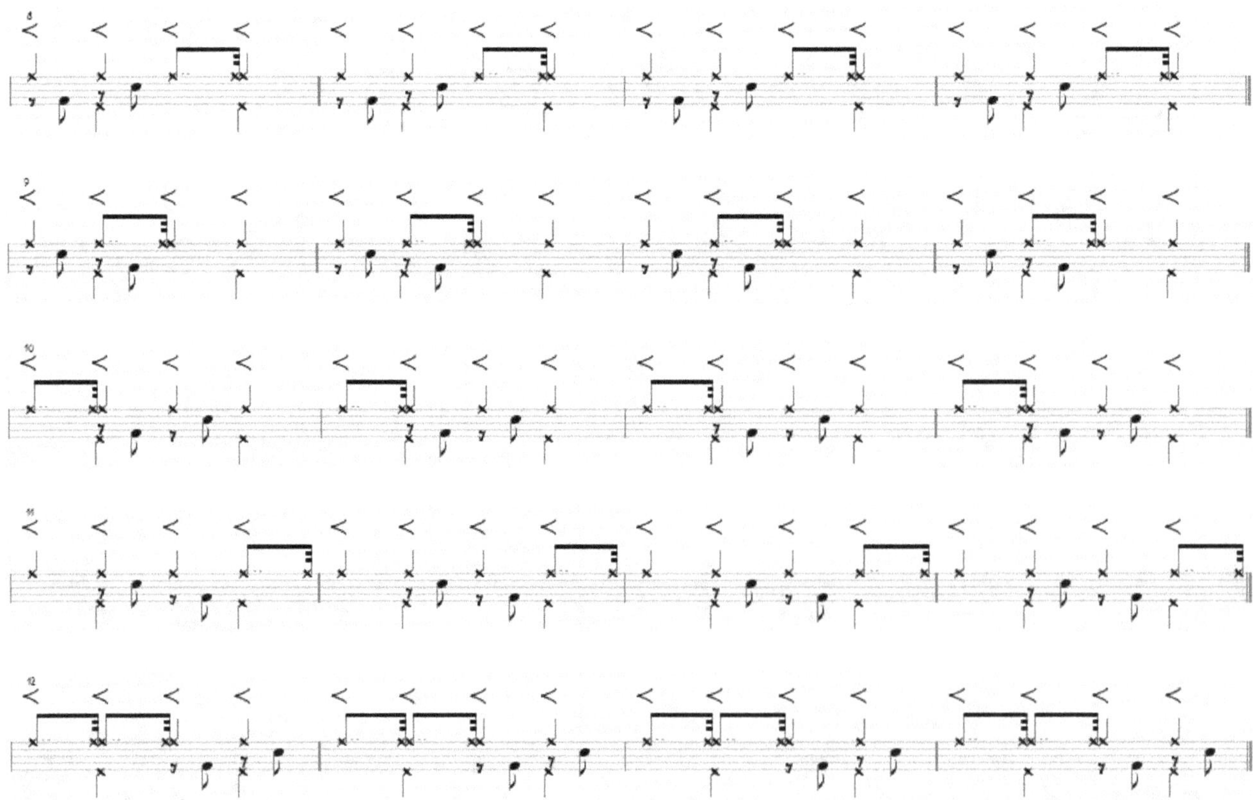

Next, play each measure from top to bottom— then from bottom to top, one measure at a time. Do this on all exercises.

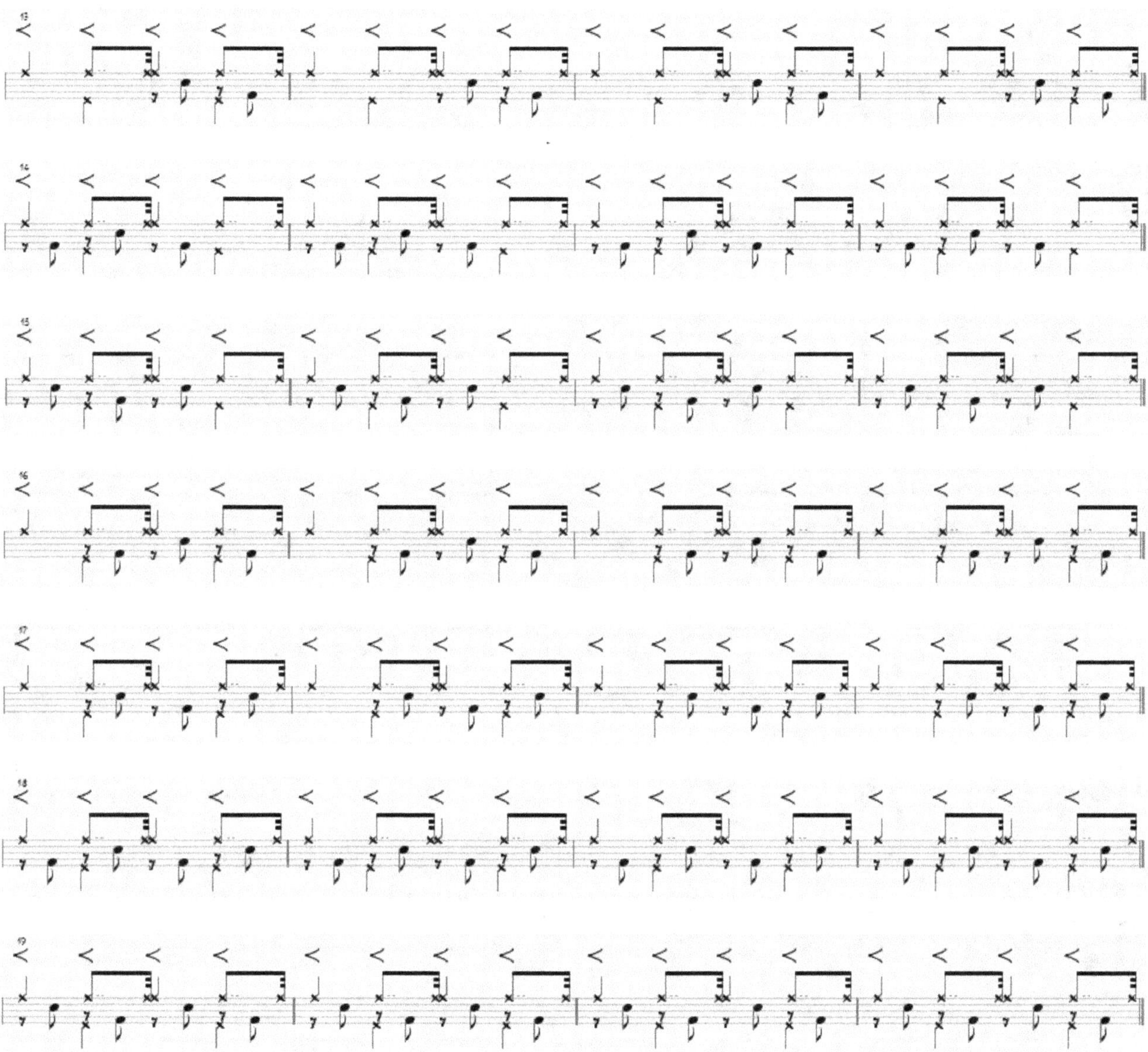

Remember to accent 1, 2, 3, 4 on the ride cymbal.

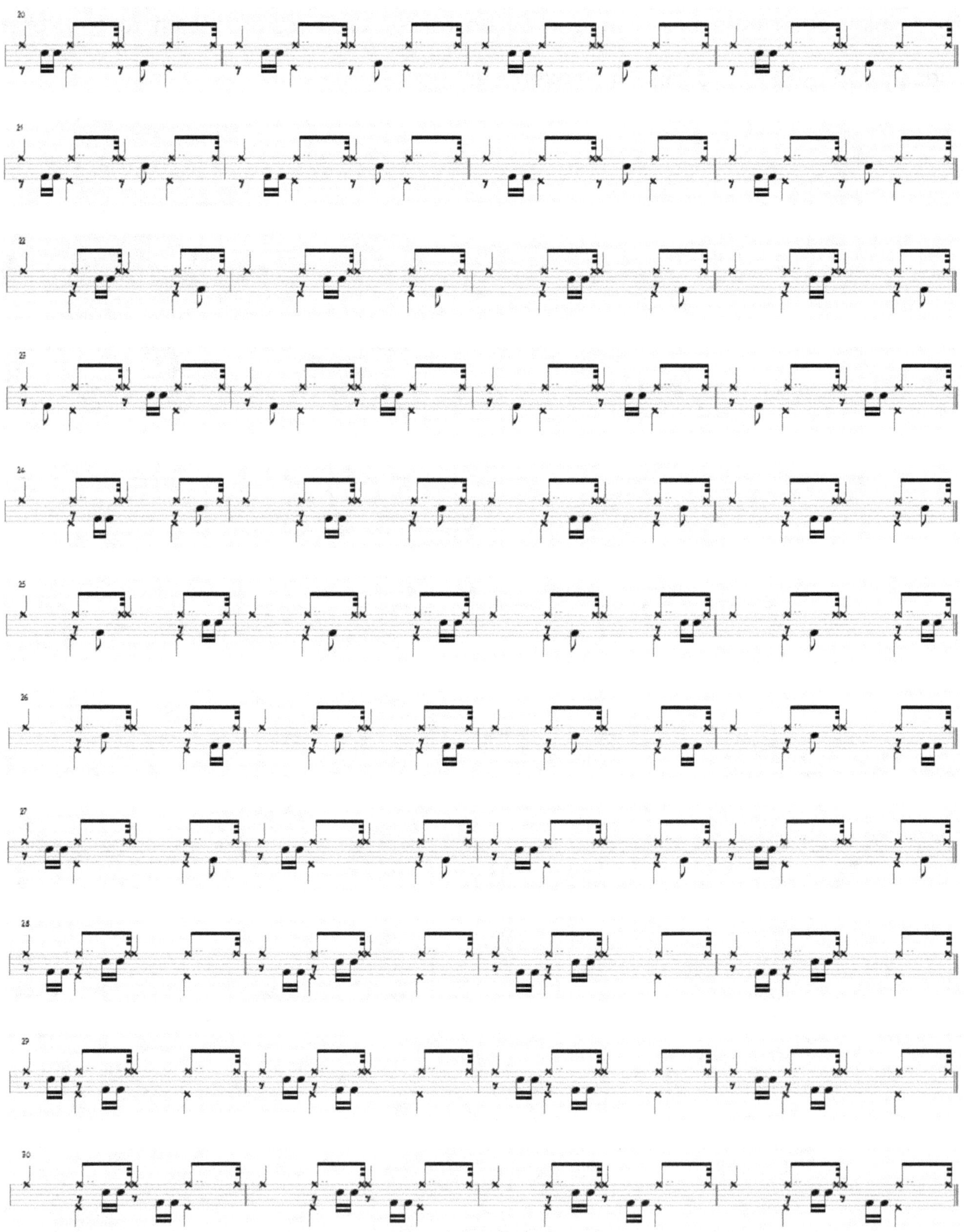

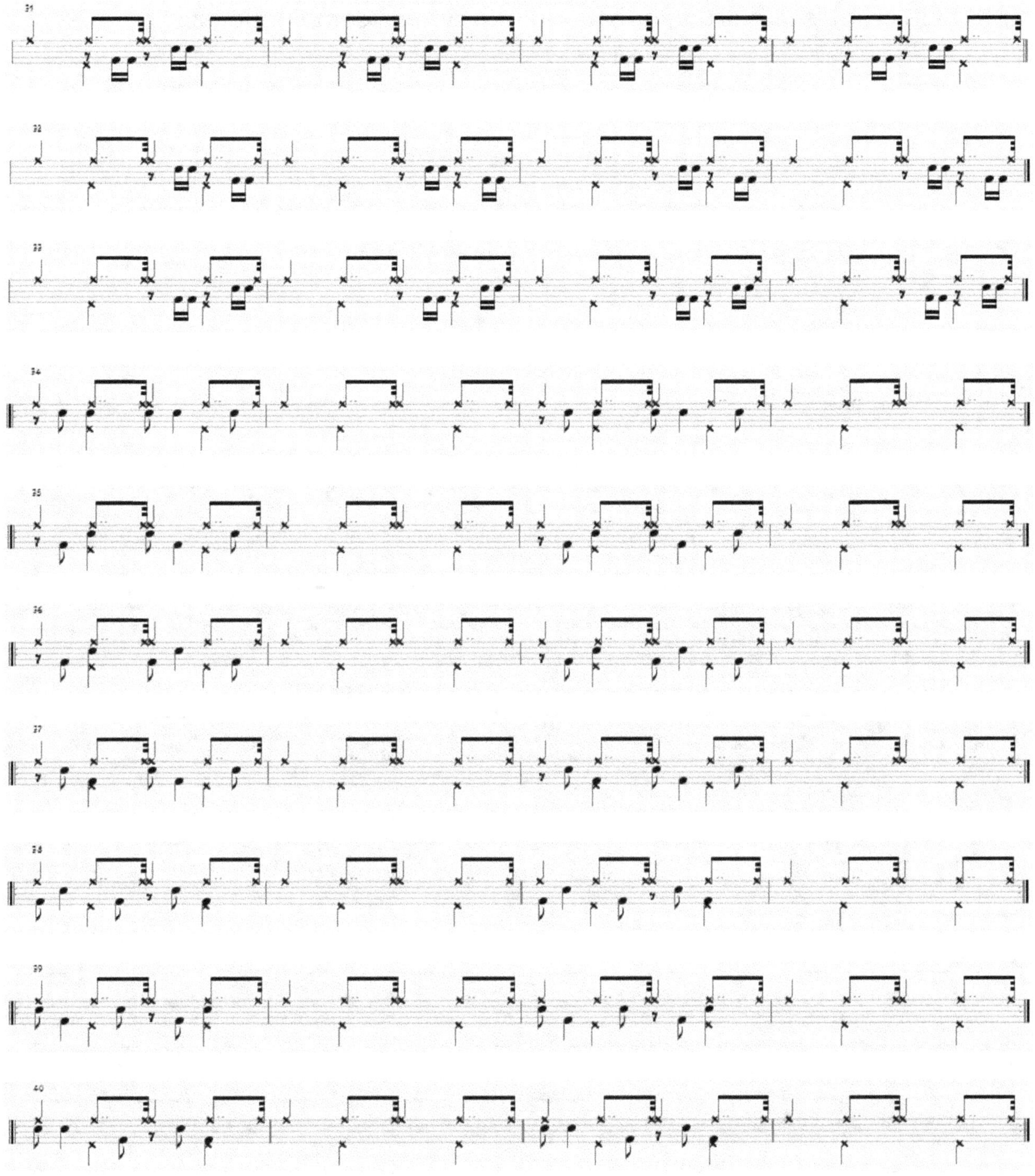

About the bass drum: Lennie liked the varied rather than consistent bass drum.

Kenny Clarke, aka Klook, played the bass drum in 4, very lightly, with an occasional

"pop." I think there is something to this, but I never checked it out.

More bass drum, snare drum, hi-hat and ride cymbal combinations:

Quarter note triplets:

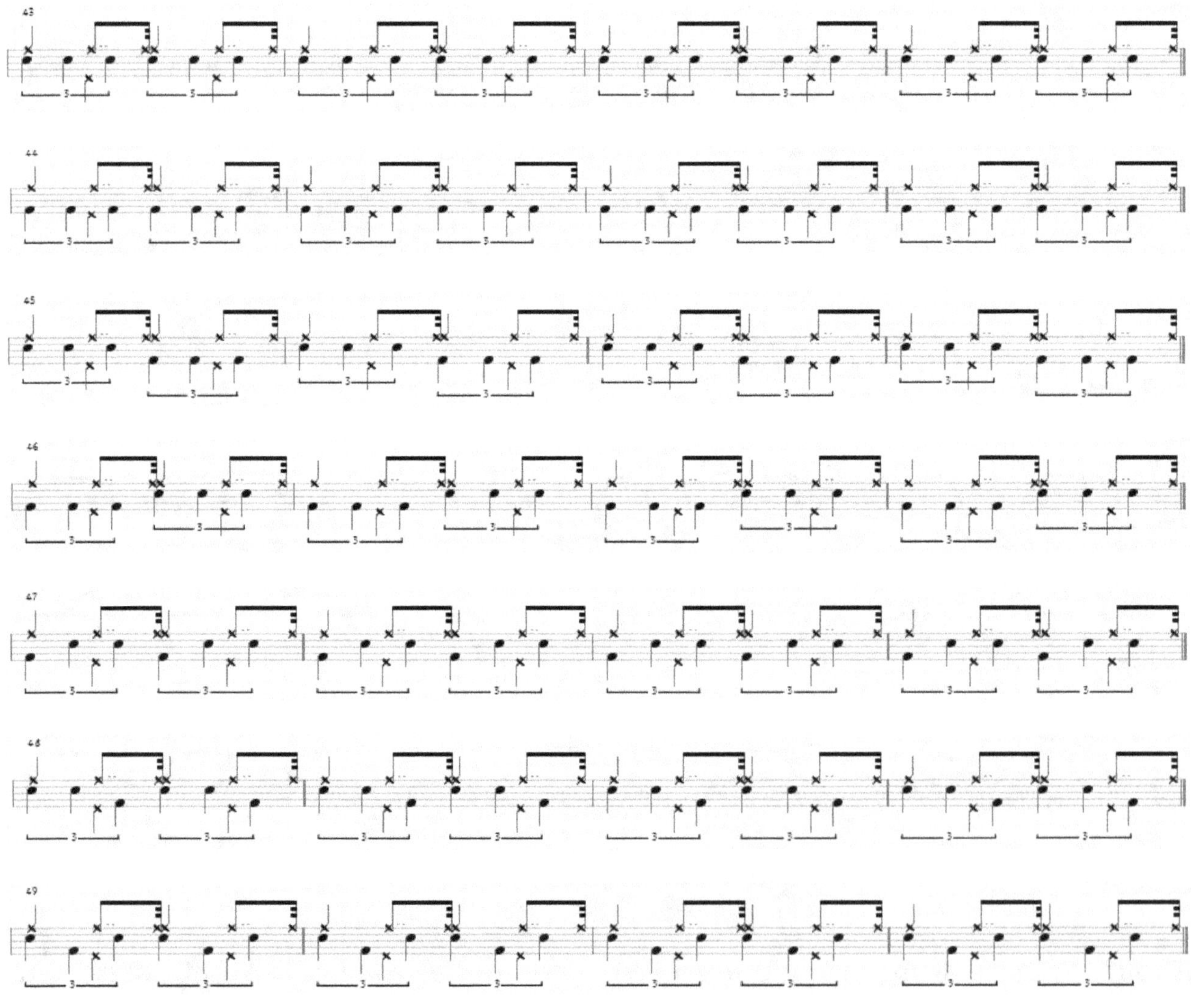

Quarter note triplets, continued.

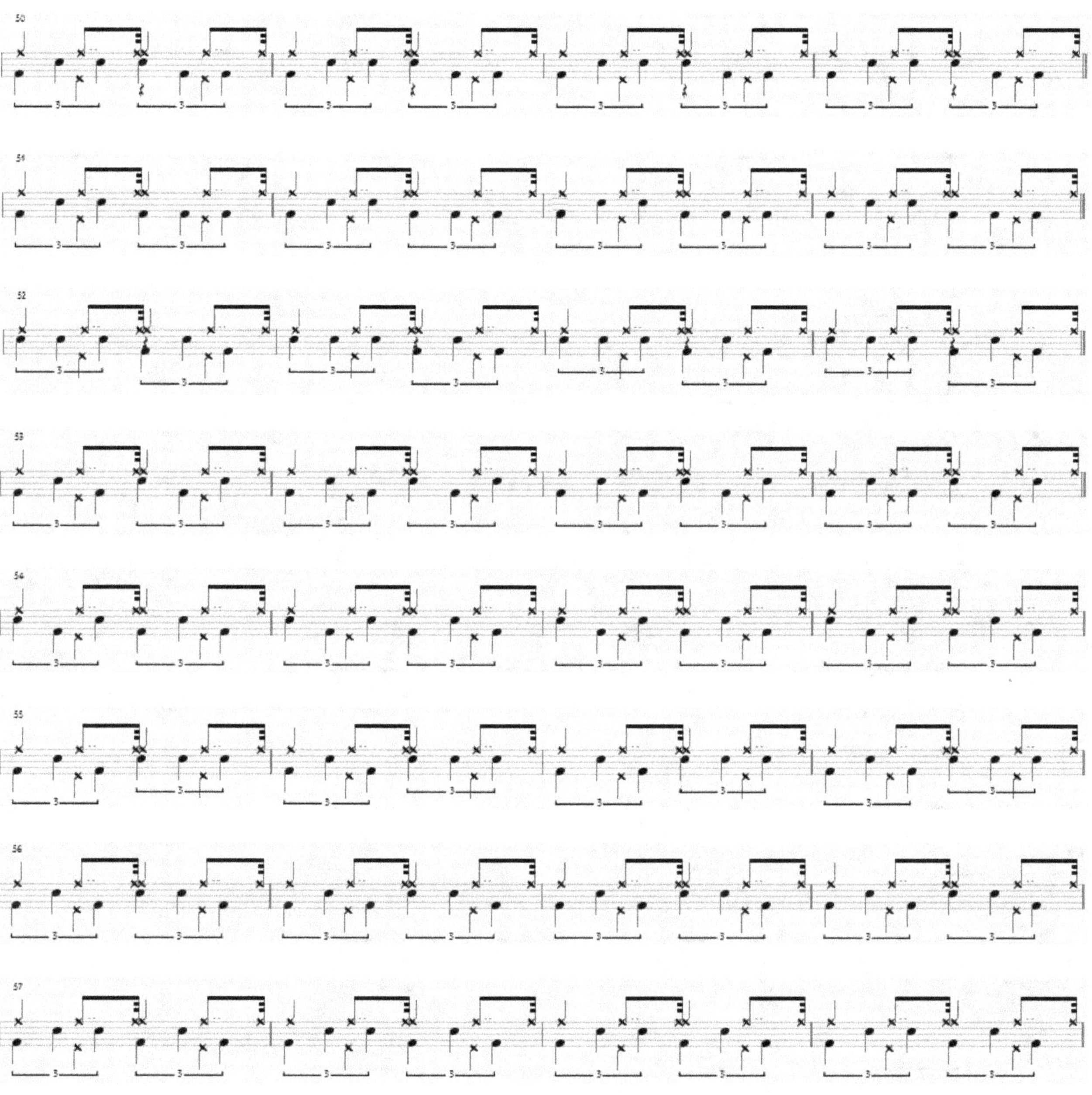

Remember, these are just exercises. When you can perform them with ease, use something like this. Eighth note triplets are also added.

Here are some exercises with a varied right hand. Remember to accent 1, 2, 3, 4.

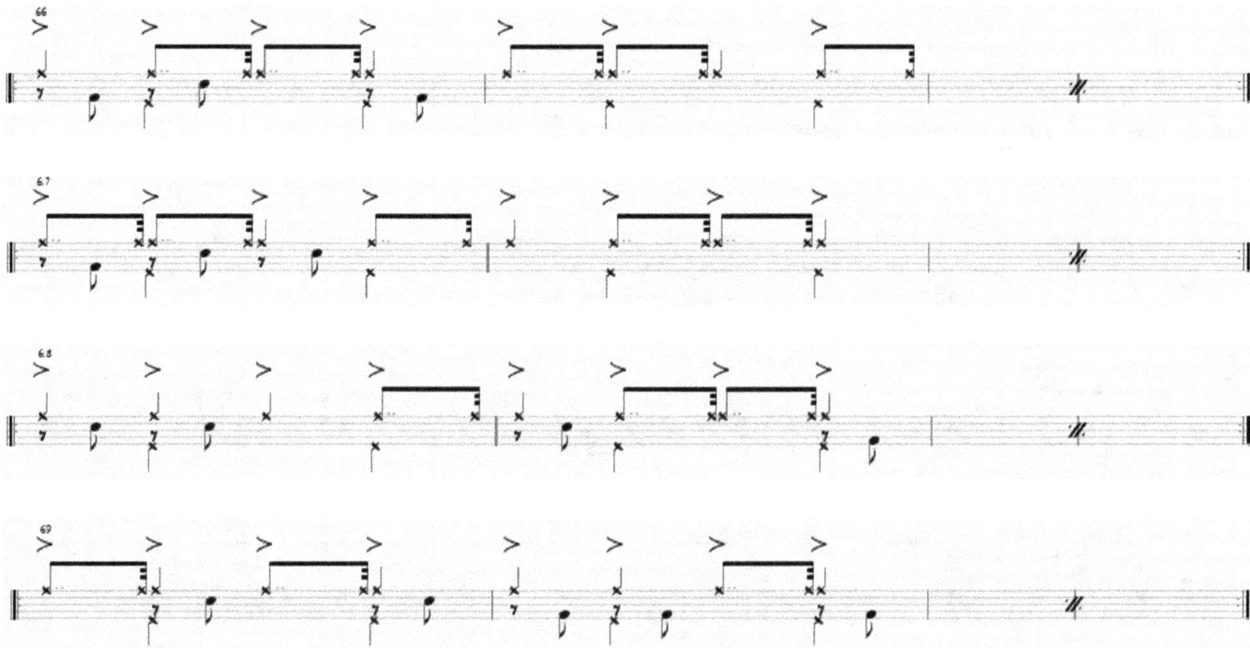

Play these exercises slowly at first, then bring them up to a more usable speed.

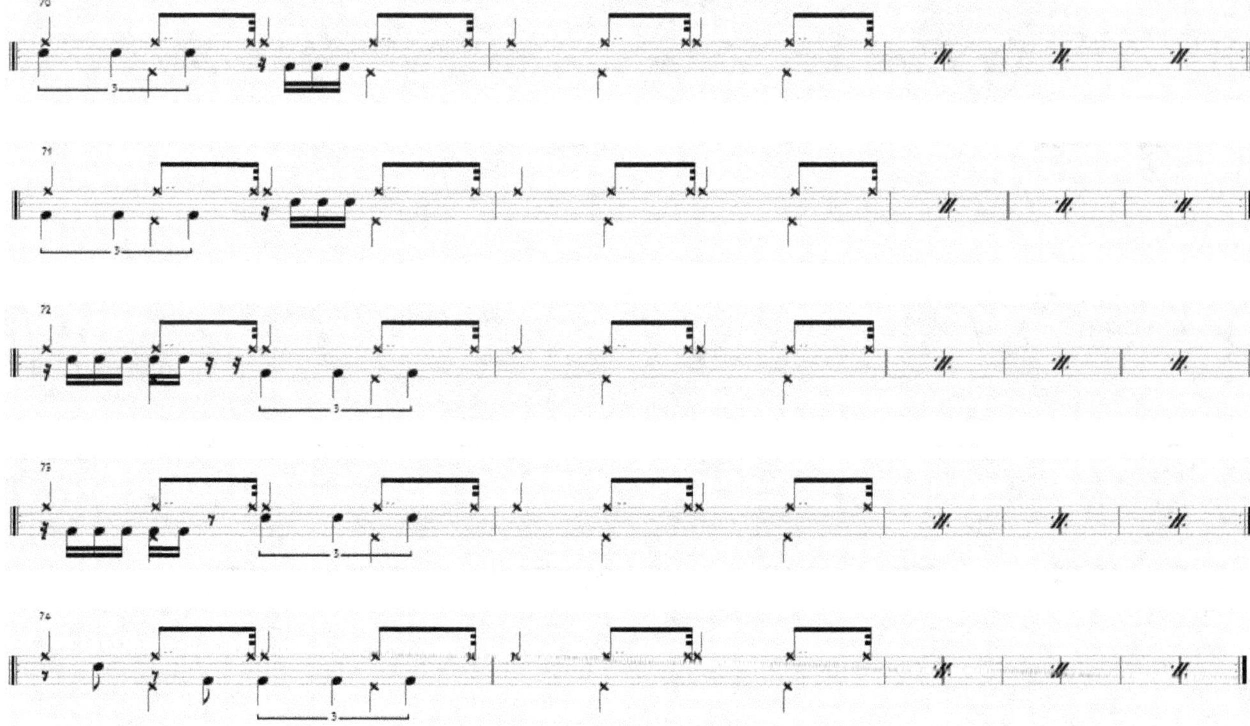

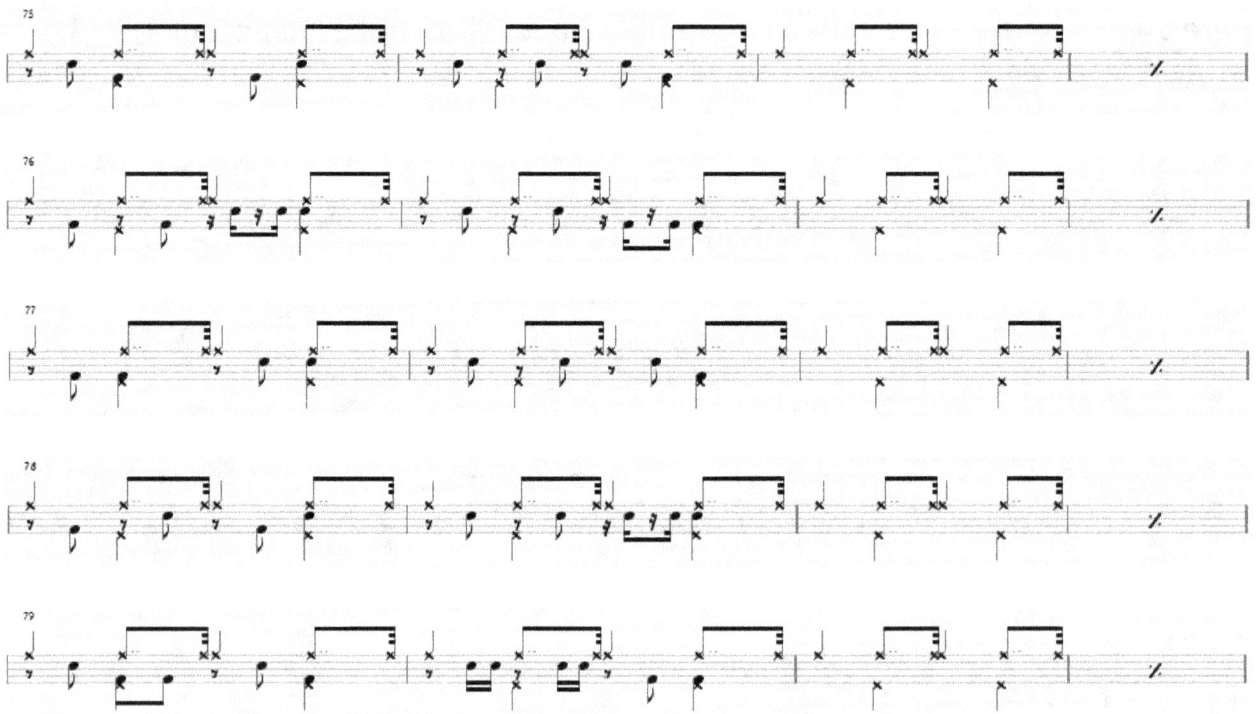

More exercises with varying ride cymbal:

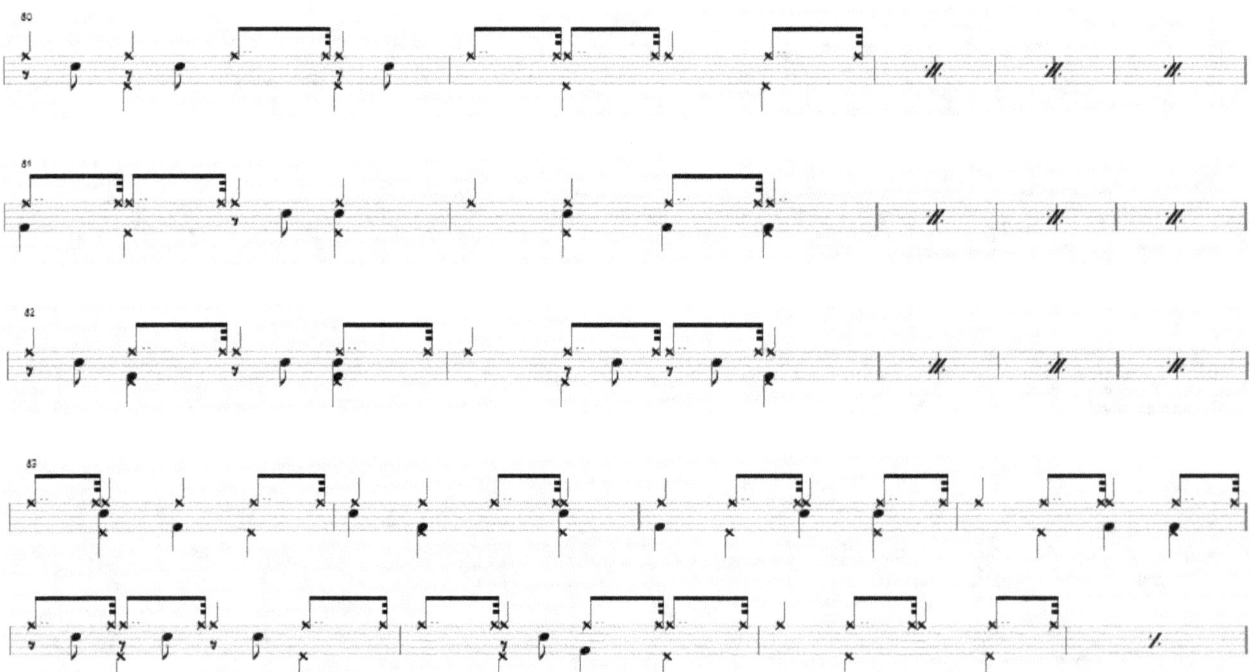

Learn all of these exercises one at a time. Bring them up to playing speed, until they flow naturally as a part of your improvising on tunes.

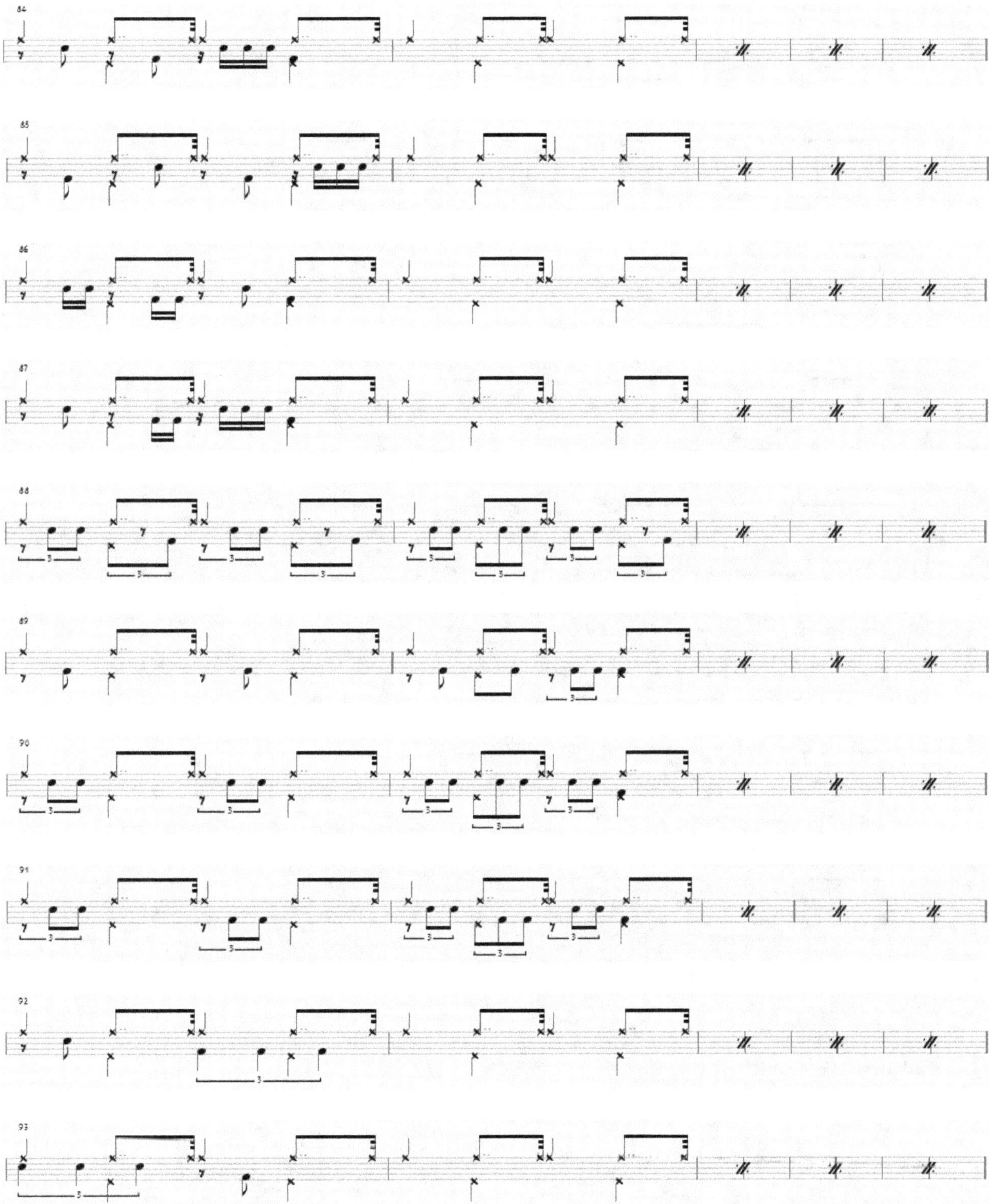

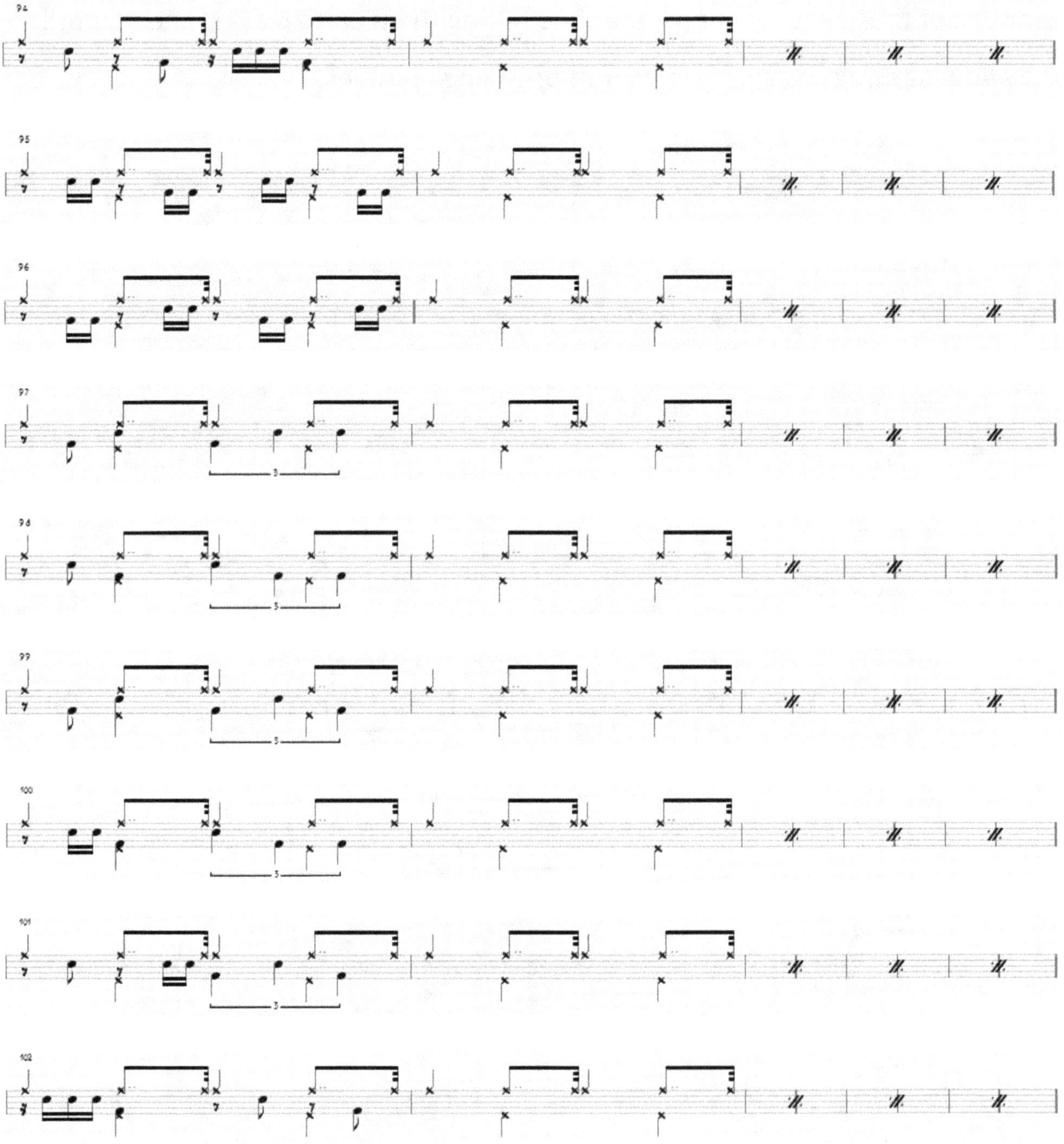

The inside-out triplet, plus.

i.e.   Usually--

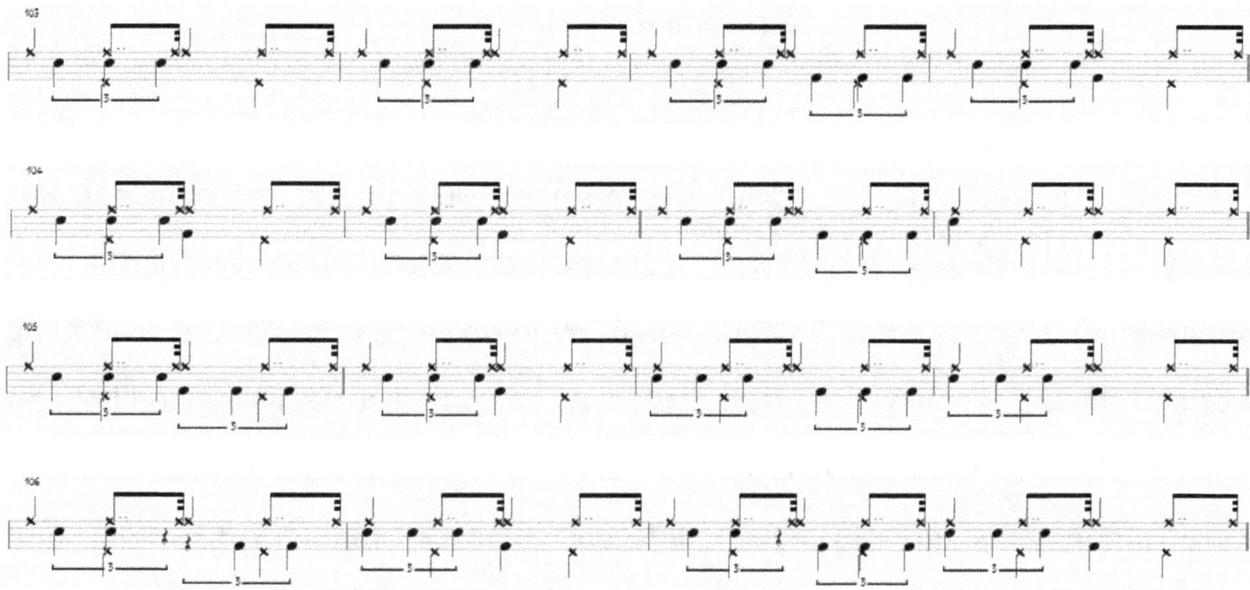

Remember, if any of these examples feel uncomfortable, don't use them; they will shake your time. Pick and choose. Use a metronome to verify your time. Eventually your beats 1, 2, 3, 4 should match its clicks.

Play the pages from top to bottom. Put a line through the patterns that you don't want, and if you need, add your own in its place to keep the time even. The exercises held in abeyance should eventually be learned, to rectify a difficulty in your playing... slowly at first, then up to where it can be played smoothly.

There are certainly more exercises that can be utilized, but work these until they become natural. These are just tools to be perfected. Once they are perfected, let them flow out with tunes until they become as truly as possible part of the tune. Strive for the ultimate—you, the tune, the group, the music—eventually one.

I studied with Lennie Tristano about 58 years ago (1960) for about 8 years and was also good friends with Joe Morello (though our points of view varied). Our disagreements were Lennie Tristano versus everyone else in the entire drumming world. After all, Lennie was a piano player. At any rate, I certainly needed help on my side (PS, even though you didn't agree, I love you, Joe Morello. You certainly were among the greatest—just different than Tristano's drummers, and apparently, so were most drummers).

But try to imagine a blind piano player teaching me how to play drums. Of course, guys like Jeff Morton, Lennie's daughter and others including myself came from Lennie's teachings—they were great players, and I was asked by Lennie to be his drummer.

I was good friends with Joe Morello before his stint with Brubeck. We picked up again later and continued our discussion about the Tristano method versus the rest of the drumming world. I quit the discussion— outnumbered over the years— but maintained my beliefs. It's a moot point now that Lennie is gone and so is Joe, and I can't play anymore. Although there is a piano player who studied with Tristano and sounds like the Tristano bag. He taught at Berklee and his name is Dave Frank. He now has his own schools on E. 52nd St and W. 30th St in New York City. I found on my computer that Skip Scott is playing drums with him— I played with his mother Betty Scott and Lloyd Lifton. I was so glad to learn about Skip. I think I gave him some lessons too. Lloyd was Lennie's "business manager" and piano student (over 20 years). He played with me and Skip's mother, who sang. Lloyd was the leader of the group. I think Tibor Tomka was the bass player. I moved to Florida. Betty Scott died. She and Lloyd made separate single albums in N.Y. Lennie played for Betty on her album. Lloyd died shortly afterward, and surprisingly, so did the young Tibor Tomka. Tibor coincidentally died in Florida. Lloyd was on his way here, but I never heard from him again. He used to come down for a week or so. We used to play every day while he was here. I rented an upright piano for when he played at my home. Walter Ellefson was the bass player. He is also gone.

Before studying with Lennie Tristano, I played in Paris with Don Byas (a wonderful man, gentle and kind... he told me he was part Native American Indian as I am) and Bill Coleman (also very kind even though at first I didn't know a particular tune with all kinds of stops and gos, sorry Bill and thanks), plus some fine French players like Andre Persiani, Guy Lafitte, etc. At the time, "Les Trois Maillets" was the Jazz spot for my area, so that's mostly where I played. I also played on the right bank at the Blue Note. I think they made a movie there with Dexter Gordon.

Klook, Kenny Clarke, always kindly acknowledged me as part of the regular players, but I was more of a student at the Sorbonne and only played when I could. Once when a visiting group Art Blakey and the Jazz Messengers came to play, Blakey opened with a long solo. Klook looked at me and said a long D-A-M-N. For my money, Klook was the best of the best. Later I found out that he played and recorded with Lennie, Lee Konitz, et al.

I was a student of the French language at the Sorbonne, to maintain my stay in France. Mme Stourdzé was my French grammar teacher and Mme Greffier was my phonetics teacher. I finished first in my class and was told by Mme Stourdzé that with two more years of study, I would have my Master's degree and I could teach French to the foreign born at the Sorbonne. However, I had to return home because a young aunt of mine was killed, or died of something strange, in her bathtub.

Before that, I was in England where Max Abrams of the BBC got me jobs playing shows across the street from the Windmill "Theatre" (English spelling), and the Winter Garden Theatre in Bournemouth where I played all kinds of top acts with singers like Jimmy Young, Yana, and other performers-- a juggler, a comedian, etc. Having little time (a few minutes) to rehearse the acts, the comedian told me (while a line outside backed up for several blocks) that when he flipped his hat with his cane and caught it with his foot, I was to give him two rim shots, one for each move. Of course, I hadn't seen the act before, so I was just watching and didn't play the rim shots. Naturally the comedian had to do something with the silence, so he said, "Remember, Sticks, we rehearsed that before the show—my cap falls and two rim shots." The audience roared. Then the comedian explained that I had just arrived, that's why they were held up outside, and Sticks just had a few minutes to run through the acts. I laughed. The theatre applauded. Then he added slowly, "I wonder why he got everyone else right but me?" The audience and I both laughed. Well, as the comedian continued with a shaggy dog story—on and on—he was about to deliver the punch line when I gave him the loudest two rim shots imaginable. I thought the audience would fall out of their seats. He later told me to take the first set of rim shots out and leave the last two in. We just laughed about it, but played it correctly from then on. All of this is just an idea of what a "Jazz" drummer had to do to stay alive. Maybe the rim shots were really subconscious anger, I don't know. I had no anger at the comedian, certainly.

While I was playing in London, Max told me to go see Phil Seaman. He used to sit in or play at the Jazz "Club American." Phil was with the Ted Heath band. I approached him and told him Max Abrams sent me over. I asked him if I could sit in. He didn't answer me. He just walked away. I guess that's understandable, just not very polite. Of course, who knows what his day was like. Later on, he was on his motorcycle with another musician, and they were both killed in a horrible accident. When I later went to Bournemouth to play, Phil's mother rented rooms there to the musicians who played at the Wintergarden Theatre. That's where I stayed! She did that as kind of a memorial to her son, so I thought. She was very sweet. My wife just read that Phil died in his flat—that's not what was going around about 60 years ago. According to Wikipedia, Phil Seamen died in 1972?? Well, maybe I got something crossed up, but I seem to remember that pretty well.

Eventually, back in New York, I played in a trio with Lennie and Sonny Dallas (bass, for you young folks), another great player gone from this world. He went to D.C. to play with Lena Horne. He needed the bucks. He was back to our trio again. Sadly, some gangsters at a Jazz club in Queens, Long Island, beat Sonny badly one night because he wouldn't play longer than the gig. He survived, and later opened a music store where he lived in Shirley on Long Island. Another fine trio that life just sucked up before it got off the ground. At 82 years old, all I can say is, I loved what I did, and of course I'm sorry life didn't let it go further. There were a few great Jazz days. Of course, one makes you want more. Some people would still be playing, but after a total of five major strokes, and several mini strokes, I have doubts. If it were up to my friend, guitarist Jimmy Young, I'd try again. Maybe I will.

I moved to Ft Lauderdale, Florida, and no one would let me sit in (union rules, they said). My wife, Susan, got transferred to Lantana, so we moved there. I went to South America with Billie Butterfield and played a few jobs with him here in Florida. Claude Kelly was the leader, and later the head of the union here. I ran a Jazz group at the New England Oyster House in Lantana with a different star each week. Of course Billie played with us there as well as Bunny Carfagno, Ron Davison, and also some locals I can't remember. I think they're all gone now anyway. I was a little younger than they.

Down here in Florida, I had to play the common triplet feel, and I just didn't enjoy it, so I started teaching and did so for about 20 years. I didn't play much, except for some rare occasions with my good friends Jim Young (guitar) and Craig Lietzke (bass)—both fine musicians.

I did make a few records. I made one recording with Jay Corre (tenor sax for Buddy Rich about 12 years) and Eddie DeMateo (great bass); and two recordings with Grammy winner, Marion Petrescu (piano) and Jamie Ousley (bass)—Wow!! Jamie teaches at the University of Miami. Marion is back at his home in Finland. I think he is one of the greatest Jazz pianists in the world, and Jamie, surely one of the greatest bassists anywhere.

Our two records on "Tie" Records can be purchased through me: Christian Buckholz, 8196 Ambach Way, Hypoluxo, FL 33462. I also have the Jay Corre record, an interesting trio—sax, bass and drums. Check out that lineup!! You can have any of the CDs for $10, or two for $15. I hate sounding so monetary but I do want you to hear them and I only have a few copies left. I will pay normal continental U.S. postage. Tell me what you think of the records.